D1756642

BE WITH ME TODAY

BE WITH ME TODAY

Prayers of Encouragement and Celebration

SAINT ANDREW PRESS
Edinburgh

First published in 2009 by
SAINT ANDREW PRESS
121 George Street
Edinburgh EH2 4YN

Copyright © Saint Andrew Press, 2009

ISBN 978 0 7152 0930 1

All rights reserved. No part of this publication may be reproduced or
transmitted in any form or by any means, electronic or mechanical,
including photocopy, recording, or information storage and retrieval
system, without permission in writing from the publisher. This book
is sold subject to the condition that it shall not, by way of trade or
otherwise, be lent, resold, hired out or otherwise circulated without the
publisher's prior consent.

The right of the Office for Worship and Doctrine, the Church of
Scotland to be identified as author of this work has been asserted in
accordance with the Copyright, Designs and Patents Act 1988.

British Library Cataloguing in Publication Data
A catalogue record for this book is available from the British Library.

It is the publisher's policy to only use papers that are natural and
recyclable and that have been manufactured from timber grown
in renewable, properly managed forests. All of the manufacturing
processes of the papers are expected to conform to the environmental
regulations of the country of origin.

Typeset in Berkeley by Waverley Typesetters, Fakenham
Printed and bound in Great Britain by Bell & Bain Ltd, Glasgow

Contents

How to use this book

The prayers in this book address contemporary life, with all its anxieties and things to celebrate. Even when we are engaged with family, friends or a wider community we can often feel alone: we hope that the prayers will enable you to acknowledge the presence of God no matter what your particular circumstances are.

You can start at the beginning and work your way to the end, or you can look through the prayers to find a particular topic you would like to address at a particular time, or you can simply pick a prayer at random and reflect on its theme. The chosen path is entirely up to you.

Some of the prayers have Scripture Readings, which are there for further reflection or to allow prayer groups to discuss the themes in relation to both the scriptures and the contemporary world.

There are some prayer activities, too. These are designed to stimulate your many senses in a prayerful way. They are perhaps best used when you are alone, when you have some time away from the routine of daily life. It may be useful to create a 'prayer corner': some personal place where you can have as much peace and quiet for reflection as you possibly can. The prayer activities hope to prompt a personal response; but prayer groups also may find that they are appropriate. You are, of course, encouraged to be creative with them, to adapt them to your own circumstances. The point is to engage with prayer, not to let it be a dull ritual.

As the prayers in this book concentrate on contemporary life, we hope you will return to them again and again and find new resonance within.

Needless Anxiety

Do not be anxious about food and drink to keep you alive and about clothes to cover your body.

~ Matthew 6:25 ~

Prayer for Reflection

Today,
I will be grateful for changing things:
    for cloud patterns
    and seasonal landscapes;
    for the restless sea
    and multi-coloured earth;
    for branch and leaf
    and fruit and flower;
    for rocks, weather carved,
    like an old face which could tell stories;
    for wind and water
    and all that was never meant to stand still.

This is your fashion-show, Lord,
better than anything humanity could ever put on.
There is no competition.

Prayer on Today's Theme

Here is a gaping sore, Lord:
    half the world diets,
        the other half hungers;
    half the world is housed,
        the other half homeless;
    half the world pursues profit,
        the other half senses loss.

Set up your cross
in the market places of our world
to remind us of your love for the lost,
and of the maliciousness of human avarice.

Redeem our souls,
redeem our peoples,
redeem our times.

Loneliness

Turn to me and be gracious to me, for I am lonely and afflicted.

~ Psalm 25:16 ~

So many people
So much loneliness
What a mystery.

When we cross the street to avoid someone, help us to
    listen to our aversion;
Going deeper
Meditating on our reaction – is it prejudice?
What are we scared of – is it anything to do with them?
Is our avoidance a protection – and if so from what?
God, may thus our meeting again become healthier, more
    open, that I could be more honest with myself and with
    you.

God, may I now face my deep loneliness, the leper within
    me,
The parts of myself I reject, that I do not want others to
    see, even you:
Is it so bad?
How can I befriend my own feelings of inadequacy,

The parts of myself I allow to get lonely and abandoned, so
    feeding my fears
Circling around in a downward spiral?

May I let you confront the parts of me that feel abandoned
    and check their reality
What I can change,
What I cannot change.
And may I have the wisdom to know the difference,
And the prayerfulness to dare to know myself,
Accept myself, open myself
Naked to your enfolding love,

Trusting you to bring the comfort that I need – and the
    challenge.   AMEN.

Prayer Activity

Most of the miracle stories of Jesus include some healing
of emotions and bring social inclusion to people who were
outcast. Think of any situation in which you feel lost, lonely,
isolated, inadequate or misunderstood. Ask Christ to bring
to your mind one of the miracle stories as 'medicine' for the
situation you have thought about – and ponder – let Jesus'
healing flow into you.

Jericho

Today salvation has come to this house.

~ Luke 19:9 ~

Sometimes, God, I feel left out.
I watch others worship and I think, 'I couldn't do that, I
would get it wrong.'
I see people happy and praising and I wonder why I don't
feel like that.
I look at groups of friends and want to know what makes
them liked and confident, and never lonely.

Lord, I am lonely. Sometimes my life is a lonely place to be.

Today, I pray for a moment in my life like Zacchaeus had.
I believe I could be transformed.
If you walked down my street.
If you came to my house!
If you chose me in front of others who overlook my
existence.
If you spent time with me, one to one, giving me the
opportunity to tell you who I am and realise the areas in
my life where I need redirection.

God, help me to see that you offer these things, that life,
    now.
Give me a space in this day to find my Jericho place ...
    where the walls come down,
    where I forget about the crowds and meet with you,
        just as I am.   AMEN.

Readings

Joshua 6:1–5; Psalm 139; Luke 19:1–10; 1 Corinthians 13

Prayer Activity

Can you truly, truly welcome the unexpected today and
expect God to be there? Can you recognise when you are
being encouraged and affirmed, and really, really rejoice? Can
you see God even in apparent disaster and respond instantly
– trusting that good will come again?

Darkness

*Even though I walk through the darkest valley, I will fear no evil:
for you are with me.*

~ Psalm 23:4 ~

In the dark I lie.

No light shines through the curtain, no dim image can be
 seen.
No height, no depth, no breadth.
And yet so claustrophobic.
No one but me and I am scared.

Because the darkness is all around.
Like solitary confinement,
I imagine what I cannot see.
What lurks, what might I touch if I move
And what might touch me?

The darkness feels like no way out – no way
And I am lost.

Now I understand the Psalmists song, God.
Words from the struggle, cries from the depths.

And I long to know that the darkness is not emptiness,
That it is filled with your presence, for you are with me.

Lord, hear my prayer that the darkness will not overcome;
And when the faintest of light is seen again
Let all my soul shout out in appreciation
for life and light that darkness can never put out.
In our struggle, in our loneliness, in our shame,
Christ be our light today.

Readings

Psalm 23	*Shepherding comfort*
Ezekiel 37:1–14	*Valley of dry bones*
1 John 1:5–10	*God is light*

My Companion Darkness

… for my soul is full of troubles.

~ Psalm 88:3 ~

Lord,
– why me? why this? why now?
I see the bad times coming – I pray.
The bad times come – I pray.
The bad times get worse – I pray:
and what feels like nothing happens.
Where are you, God, when I need you?
Is it something I have said, is it something I have done?
What do I have to say, what do I have to do
so that I can hear your voice and know you are with me?
Day and night – and nothing!

If only I knew the secret formula of words and actions
that unlocks your heart and prompts you to act.

Lord,
there are times when prayer is hard work,
and times when I wonder why I persevere with it.
My own needs empty my resources for living.
The needs of others drain my treasury of life.

I am left, emptied and drained, and I don't know what to
   do.
The lights go out, one by one, and darkness is my only
   companion.
Yet still I pray,
sometimes beyond reason, sometimes beyond hope,
asking again and again,
laying bare my soul,
stretching out my hands,
and believing even in this darkness
that you will hear and you will come.
Come, Lord, come!   AMEN.

Prayer Activity

New life is born out of darkness, for example, from the
womb. What part of your life 'feels dead'? Every time you
feel hopeless, alone, in darkness, make a gesture of faith –
remembering a favourite verse, Bible passage, saying a prayer,
lighting a candle, playing music, recalling the faithfulness
of God in the past. Start now with a present situation or a
memory which is still hard to bear.

Light and Darkness

Consider whether the light in you is not darkness.

~ Luke 11:35 ~

Lord,
my world is flooded with bright lights,
offering me entertainment,
persuading me to buy,
putting a shine on bad news,
claiming to show me 'reality'.
Why does it all seem so staged?
And what of the light within me?
Does it not glow and fade as the dark silhouettes of greed
    or envy,
bitterness, arrogance or self hatred chase across its
    surface?
Help me to recognise when things seem clear only because
    of my driving ambition,
when things seem so obvious only because I am not taking
    others into account,
when my light is merely darkness dressed up.
Illuminate me from within with your Word.
Make me a lantern that shows others the way:
with a generosity which spills into darkest corners,

with a level of understanding which reveals what is true,
with a strength of love which glows mid distrust and fear.

Readings

2 Samuel 22:26–30	*You are my lamp, O Lord*
Proverbs 4:18–19	*The path of the righteous is like the light of dawn*
Luke 11:33–6	*Putting the lamp on the lampstand*
John 3:18–21	*People loved darkness rather than light*
Colossians 1:11–14	*He has rescued us from the power of darkness*
2 Peter 1:19	*A lamp shining in a dark place*

Prayer Activity

Darkness does not possess the ability to remove light, but
light forces darkness to scatter. Find a dark place and sit for
a spell. Feel for the match and light the candle. Watch the
flame grow in strength. Follow the light out to the periphery,
and see how far that little light can stretch. Now kindle
Christ's light in you. Imagine it permeating your whole
body and mind, and watch it reaching out to the people and
community among whom you live.

Hope

You are my Lord: I have no good apart from you.

~ Psalm 16:2 ~

Lord, all my life and aspirations are pinned on you,
my present and my future hopes.
Even in the face of uncertainty, illness, death,
I want to hold you firm.
Then you dazzle me with the truth
that it is you who have hold of *me*, with love.
I can only thank you for the security that gives
for any situation I may know today.

Nothing will be outwith the reach of your embrace
or diminish the wealth of your resources.
That is hope for me in life and through death.
Lord, please keep me in that place of trust
and true hope, through Jesus Christ.   AMEN.

Readings

Genesis 45:4–8; Psalm 16; John 16:25–33; Philippians
1:12–26; John 14:1–7

Prayer Activity

The path of life. As you walk today, allow a text or hymn to come to your mind. Let the words find a rhythm in tune with your walking and your breath. Allow your walking to bring you life. The Psalms were often walked and sung on pilgrimage. You are finding your own way to join this ancient way of worship, of embodying God's love in you as you move and breathe.

The Lord's Prayer

Blessing

Hope for today be yours;
hope for the way be yours;
hope without end
through Christ, your friend.

Ahab and Jezebel

> He said to her, 'Because I spoke to Naboth the Jezreelite and said to him, "Give me your vineyard for money; or, if you prefer, I will give you another vineyard for it"; but he answered, "I will not give you my vineyard."' His wife Jezebel said to him, 'Do you now govern Israel? Get up, eat some food, and be cheerful; I will give you the vineyard of Naboth the Jezreelite.'
>
> ~ 1 Kings 21:6–7 ~

I want, Lord. Don't we all?
And what I want is what I don't have.
Having does not kill the butterfly *Desire*.
It flits from what I have just got, to light on what I don't have. Yet.
Desire is, I know, insatiable. It empowers me,
Just as it empowers, charges, drives, this world of conspicuous consumption.
For I am a consumer, and the consumer is king.

My desire is not outrageous or brutal, Lord. Surely my desire kills no one.
It would be satisfied with very little more than I already have.
I could say 'Enough ...' *Any time I wanted to.*

But I hear the seductive whisper
'Why settle for less?' 'You're worth it!'
I lip-know, but do not heart-know, that these things
Are no measure of who and what I am.
Not before You. But they are with me.
And still the voices whisper.
'Are you not a consumer?' 'Is the consumer not king?'

'Is it my fault if the world works this way?'
Sometimes I can manage to say it and believe it.
If consumer society empowers the consumer,
And I happen to be a consumer ...

Power is exercised in my name, Lord God, and I am
     complicit,
Because I am silent, and because I continue to consume.
My desire would consume the world.
Teach me how to decline, with proper revulsion.
Teach me what is *enough* ...

Longing

As a deer longs for flowing streams, so my soul longs for you,
O God.

~ Psalm 42:1 ~

Longing is at the centre of my life,
a hunger for food, for sex, for love.
I have a thirst to belong,
to be at home, at ease with myself, with others, with life.

I confess that I have never longed for you
in the way the writer of these religious poems has longed.
What agony! What yearning!
Yes, I recognise it, but not in such
painful depth of spirit.

> *Tears are my food day and night ...*
> *my flesh faints for you,*
> *as in a dry and weary land*
> *where there is no water.*

Lord, I have never been to these extremities:
so utterly alienated from human company,
in mortal danger from cruel enemies,
crying out for revenge, despairing of spiritual aid.

God, make haste to help those
whose misery, or harsh environment, or broken spirit
   makes them cry.
Come to their souls with peace. Answer their longing with
   belonging.
Bring them to the point where they, too, can say:

> *My soul is satisfied as with a rich feast,*
> *and my mouth praises you with joyful lips*
> *when I think of you on my bed,*
> *and meditate on you in the watches of the night;*
> *for you have been my help,*
> *and in the shadow of your wings I sing for joy.*

Readings

Psalm 42; Psalm 43; Psalm 63; Matthew 11:28; John
7:37–9; Romans 8:18–30

Lost

*He was trying to see who Jesus was, but on account of the crowd
he could not, because he was short in stature. So he ran ahead and
climbed a sycamore tree.*

~ Luke 19:3–4 ~

Feeling low in every sense, insecure in being and crushed
   by a crowd giving no recognition or care – God, we can
   imagine so well how Zacchaeus felt that day.

Confronted with his own deceit and bad track record,
   oppressed by the fear that this was how it was always
   going to be,
Zacchaeus sensed your presence as an opportunity to rise
   above.

So let us have that kind of moment today, God.
Let us climb out of the depths to see who you are,
And in our shame and worry may we find that half-way
   house,
That secure branch to grab hold of,
That safe place to sit,
until you lovingly call to us, to finally let you in.

And help us too, God, to be rooted in your strength for
   others:
To be people they lean on
Places they shelter
Life they connect to.
That they too will see Jesus – in us.   AMEN.

Prayer Activity

Hold a piece of wood in your hand. Look at its grain, its
colour, its shape. Now imagine that small piece as part of
the large tree it came from – where did it grow? What did it
look like? What happened around it? Offer a prayer now for
the Christian community you are part of – and reflect on the
tree as a symbol of the church.

Blessing

> The possibilities of forgiveness,
> The strength of life,
> The root of love
> Be shown in you this day
> For Christ's sake.

Disappointment

Do not disappoint my hope.

~ Psalm 119:116 ~

Prayer for Reflection

I sometimes think my expectations are too high!
I can even demand more from others than from myself.
– tidiness in the home,
– efficiency at work,
– consistency in politicians,
– reliability in church duties.

But then I sometimes wonder if I ever fulfil
other people's expectations of me!

I remember Jesus in the garden,
castigating God for not coming up to scratch,
but then realising that there was still something more
that he was expected to do.

Help me, Lord, not to disappoint you today.

Prayer on Today's Theme

I think of those whose relationships,
or creativity, or career,
have not matched their expectations.

I think of those whose self-esteem is low
because others remind them continually
how disappointing they've been.

But I think too of the father
who saw the approach of the son
    who had been such a disappointment,
and ran and embraced him,
and welcomed his lost child home.

Remind them all, and remind me,
that your love will always exceed all expectation.

.

Fear – a Man Released from Torment

He had often been fettered and chained up …

~ Mark 5:4 ~

Lord God,
fear comes in many guises into our lives.
It is legion:
the fear of the unknown
which blights our vision,
the fear of pain
which narrows our world,
the fear of failure
which challenges our confidence.

When such fear comes, we are in fetters, we are in chains.
Fear comes to war-torn lands;
fear comes to homes where hunger stalks;
fear comes to the lonely, the frail, the dispossessed.

When such fear comes,
blotting out the sunlight hope of well-lived life,
come to our rescue
and help us through fears seen, and unseen,
that we might be set free

to walk and live and love unhindered,
acknowledging your power to cast out fear
through your perfect love for us all.   AMEN.

Readings

1 Kings 19:9–18; Isaiah 35; Isaiah 43:1–7; Matthew
14:22–7; Mark 5:1–20; 1 John 4:7–21

Silence

Prayer Activity

Feel the earth beneath your feet or feel the chair beneath you.
Sense the solidity and be glad of the security. Remain with
that feeling for a few minutes. Ask God to remind you of this
solidity whenever you face difficulties.

Temptation

Do not put us to the test, but save us from the evil one.

~ Matthew 6:13 ~

Prayer for Reflection

Sometimes, Lord,
it amazes me
how I sat examinations
in my childhood,
harder ones in my youth,
developed my proficiency,
    my skills
being tested all the time,
and aiming to succeed.
And yet despite all this effort,
and even proof of passing the test,
in the dilemmas of daily life,
experience has not bred expertise.
From the trite answer,
    the easy solution,
    the careless response
and all such allurements,
Good Lord, deliver me.

Prayer on Today's Theme

Lord Jesus Christ,
you have harried hell,
detoxified darkness,
and conquered the powers of wickedness.
Confront today
those who consort with what is evil,
    who misuse money,
    exploit the vulnerable,
    trade in malicious gossip,
    or demean their own bodies.

Shout at them,
as loudly as you shouted at Lazarus,
that they may walk away from death
and come to you for cleansing.

Abraham and Isaac

'Take your son, your only son Isaac, whom you love, and go to the land of Moriah, and offer him there as a burnt offering on one of the mountains ...'

~ Genesis 22:2 ~

If love is a good thing, why is it tested?
If family is so sacred, why is it hard?
If parenting is precious, why is it painful?
If you, God, always provide,
Why do we sometimes feel we will lose everything?

Thinking of Isaac; innocently asking 'Where is the lamb for
    the sacrifice?'
We offer our prayers today for vulnerable children
In our time, naive and trusting.

Thinking of Abraham; following without question,
Acting without hesitation, strangely focused
We offer our questions, our doubts and discomfort.

Thinking of Jesus; your only son,
Given to die because you loved us so much,
Christ who asks us to follow in costly ministry –

We ask today,
What is the cost?
What are the sacrifices we are prepared to make?

Prayer Activity

Call to mind a relationship or situation where there is a lack
of trust. Offer your concerns and your questions about this
to God.

Blessing

> God,
> of immeasurable love
> of family beyond convention
> of trust beyond understanding
> bless through Christ your given son.   AMEN.

Humdrum Relationships – Sarah and Abraham

> But Abram said to Sarai, 'Your slave-girl is in your power; do to her as you please.' Then Sarai dealt harshly with her, and she ran away from her.
>
> ~ Genesis 16:6 ~

Sometimes, Lord, we know,
There is an incredible harshness to day-to-day life.
Hopes, expectations, dangerous dreams,
Grind together and shatter; love turns to hate, people
behave very badly.
Shards and sharp edges wound and lacerate.

Life can be like that.
We dare not idealise, especially not in the name of faith,
As though life had to be simplified to fit our small vision
of you.

That you in your faithfulness and love are gracious where
we are not –
Is this not the heart of our faith? And if it is not, Lord, let
it be.

Sarai was insecure; Abram was weak; this is how they were.
From spat to vendetta, was this the family of your exalted
  promise?
Is this soap opera really the story of your covenant?
Help us to turn the question round, Lord.
'Does God really love real people?'
'Can God really love unlovable people?'

Free us from sanitised versions of faith.
Free us from that sundering of God from human reality
That makes us censors of the story.
Free us from the dark suspicion
That you can only deal with the nice, respectable bits of us,
Or that God is prim and easily shocked.
Challenge us with your realism, that sees us as we are,
And deals with that.

Prayer Activity

Take a mirror. Look into it. Who do you see? What do you
know about who you see? Knowing what you know, can you
love and accept what you see? Can you see someone whom
God loves? Now visualise someone with whom you have
difficulties getting on. See their face framed in the mirror. Ask
the same questions. Bring the answers honestly to God.

Praying

'This is how you should pray: Our Father in heaven …'

~ Matthew 6:9 ~

Prayer for Reflection

It is prayer time again, Lord,
time to bring you my shopping list,
'Do this, fix that, and, oh yes, bring peace to the world.'
So much I ask Lord, and how self-centred I sound.
But you have taught me how to pray,
    to find space and time to hear your voice,
    to be still and know that you are God.

You have already told us the secret of prayer,
how we needn't adopt special postures,
or use particular words,
nor wait for emergencies,
but how we must walk with you,
    be guided by you, be lived in by you,
    listen for you day and night,
– indeed, say *Our Father* …

Prayer on Today's Theme

Lord, stretch out towards those who cannot pray:
those for whom prayer is merely a routine,
those who use prayer as a substitute for action,
those who are proud of their prayers,
those whose prayers do not carry over into daily life,
those who feel no-one prays for them,
those who feel they have no-one to pray to.

Drama

The storm was raging unabated, and our last hopes of coming through alive began to fade.

~ Acts 27:20 ~

Prayer for Reflection

Thank you, Lord, for a Gospel
not only found in the quiet, devotional moment,
    when the mind can appreciate it at leisure,
but encountered in the dramas of life,
    when body and mind together
    grapple with tensions and troubles
    and grasp for something to hold on to.

Teaching patiently on a hillside,
listening thoughtfully in a kitchen,
praying in a garden,
    but also head to head with the Pharisees,
    in the cut and thrust of the court room,
    in the face of the shouting crowd,
    in the agony of execution,
you, Jesus, lived out the Gospel.

Be with me today
    when the hours hang heavy
    or when things are happening so fast
    that there is no time even to think.

Prayer on Today's Theme

I pray for those whose day will be full of drama,
    facing a sheriff,
    going through an operation,
    waiting for news,
    being involved in an accident,
    discussing a divorce settlement,
and all those also who wish
    something would happen to them.

Let them feel your arms around them,
    that they may not sink.

My Health

'Do you want to be made well?'

~ John 5:6 ~

Prayer for Ourselves

A centurion ran to catch you and plead for his servant;
a man cried out to you as his daughter lay dying;
a woman risked humiliation, reaching out to you through
   the crowd,
that she might be healed.
Yet, the man by the pool seemed to bask in his misery,
as others stepped, and jumped, and dived into the waters
   of new life.
Whenever I feel sorry for myself, Lord, cajole me out of my
   lethargy.
When I shrink back,watching others grasp for hope,
make me rise up and plunge into your love.

Prayer for Others

Christ, healer,
by your wisdom,
guide the environmentalist,

the researcher, the scientist,
all who seek to bring us healthy surroundings in which to
    live.

By your grace,
teach us to value each person we encounter,
in spite of the prejudice bred within us
about disability,
particular diseases,
our misunderstandings about illness of the mind.

In your strength, Lord,
enable us all to look after ourselves,
in what we consume, what we do, how we live,
that so exercised in body, mind, and spirit,
we might be all that we can be.

Straight and Narrow

Narrow is the gate and constricted the road that leads to life, and those who find them are few.

~ Matthew 7:14 ~

Prayer for Reflection

Sometimes,
like a blindfold woman
trying to put a tail on the donkey,
I rely on my skill
and end up wide of the mark.
And sometimes,
like a drunk man making for home,
I end up walking in circles.
... and this,
not so much to do with my sense of direction
as with the way I go astray
when it comes to faith, hope, and love.
All the time that I rely on my own skill,
I fail to lean on and learn from you, my Saviour.

God give me the grace which I lack
to find the direction my life is meant for.

Prayer on Today's Theme

A thought
for those who knowingly lead others
up the garden path ...

A thought
for those who deliberately persuade others
that everybody should do what they like ...

A thought
for those who intentionally tell others
that freedom should have no limits,
even if it infringes on someone else's life.
Show them your cross, Lord Christ:
ultimate freedom without limit,
but ultimately reached by a narrow road.

Martha

But Martha was distracted by her many tasks ...

~ Luke 10:40 ~

O God, we often look on the appearance but you look on
the heart.
Forgive us for our superficial judgments, our casual
dismissal of some people.
Give us the seeing eye and the understanding mind.

Help us this day to think of Martha – not as the moaning
servant but
one who receives Jesus into her house;
one who, recognising his authority, appeals to Jesus;
one who, at the death of Lazarus, goes out to meet him;
one who asserts that Jesus is the divine physician;
and one to whom Jesus declares that he is the
resurrection and the life.
O God, help us to learn from her fuller story and to affirm
as she did
that Jesus is the Christ, the Son of God.

Lord Jesus Christ, who stands at the door, may I receive
you into my home ...

Lord of the pots and pans, the plane and lathe, calm me
    when trauchled . . .
Lord, good physician, soothe my spirit, allay my anxieties,
    restore and renew me in my worship and work . . .
Lord, conqueror of death, with me in my living and
    striving,
with me in my dying, raise me with all who serve.   AMEN.

Prayer Activity

Traditionally many of us say grace before a meal. Try to write
your own. Find ways to include in it an acknowledgment
of the difficult parts of your day as well as thanks for the
moments of delight.

False Pride

People who are proud will soon be disgraced. It is wiser to be modest.

~ Proverbs 11:2 ~

Prayer for Reflection

I believe, Lord,
that you intended me to like myself,
even to love myself.

Otherwise how could I expect others
to love the 'me' I refuse to cherish?

And, in any case, filled with self-loathing,
what goodness could I share
in your name?

But pride – that's something else when it prevents me from
  seeing
    anyone else but me,
when it presumes a perfection
    I have never achieved.

For self respect, prepare me;
from false pride, protect me.

Prayer on Today's Theme

Today, Lord,
I remember those whose position of authority
might tempt their pride:
    politicians, civil servants,
    lawyers, accountants,
    and all confidants
    and keepers of secrets.

Prevent them from abusing
    the trust their position affords them;
and should the heights of responsibility
    distort their vision,
help them, like you,
to become human.

Patience

I waited patiently for the Lord; he inclined to me and heard my cry.

~ Psalm 40:12 ~

Lord,
we find it so hard to be patient in our world.
We want everything immediately:
instant credit, instant meals, instant entertainment, instant
   relationships, even.

No, we don't want to wait; we want it NOW!

Yet the Scriptures are full of people waiting –
in stillness, in hope, in longing,
waiting for your promises to become reality,
waiting for the dawn of your Kingdom,
waiting for you to act ...

You would remind us that the waiting time,
the time of 'Yes ... but not yet ...'
is the learning and growing time.

You would call us to action in waiting,
being active in your service,
being busy about our Father's business as we await your
    Kingdom's dawning …

Today I remember all who wait –
the oppressed, the exploited, the anxious, the grieving.
May they find you in their waiting time.

Prayer Activity

Mental relaxation in God's presence can be a form of patient prayer. The discipline is one of relaxing the mind and waiting. Practise this kind of praying. Allow yourself to relax and to enter into the experience. Taking time simply 'to be' can sometimes help us to become more aware of the wonder and vitality of life's gifts.

Comfort

Even though I walk through the darkest valley, I fear no evil.

~ Psalm 23:4 ~

Prayer for Ourselves

By the word of a neighbour
    you comfort me;
through a letter from a friend
    you comfort me;
in the kindness of a stranger
    you comfort me;
in many and unexpected ways
    you comfort me each day
and give me strength to face the way ahead.

Prayer for Others

Lord, help me be a comforter to others,
    to listen and not always to speak,
    to understand more and judge less,
    to build up and not put down.
May the church, in Jesus' name,
offer healing and comfort,

consolation and peace,
and fresh hope for tomorrow,
to all who are lonely:
those cut off from others because of their success,
those isolated through rumours and gossip,
those separated because of their high office,
those disregarded because they have little,
those who espouse an unpopular cause.
May all find strength in your divine friendship.

Discipline

*We are disciplined to renounce godless ways ... looking forward to
the happy fulfilment of our hope.*

~ Titus 2:12–13 ~

Prayer for Reflection

It will come anyhow –
the time when you bring all things
    to a magnificent finale.
But you have not called me
    to hang around till it happens,
    to wait in the wings,
    and to appear on cue.
I am to help accustom those I live amongst –
    to begin to move with your step,
    and to mouth the words all will later sing.

But, Lord, for others to be convinced I must practise,
so that I know the steps and have the song by heart.

Help me to be disciplined and to learn, from Scripture,
    from prayer,
and by listening to fellow Christians,

what we shall become when all things are fulfilled
and you are Lord of all.

Prayer on Today's Theme

I pray for the Church, when we feel our grasp is adequate
 but really we are relying on rusty memories
 of what we once learned in Sunday School;
when we feel we do not need to search Scripture,
 study those who have wrestled with the faith,
 learn from the giants of prayer in our tradition,
 or listen to the voices of today.

Help us all to discipline ourselves,
assessing how we fall short,
giving account to each other of our faith,
 our prayer,
 and how we live our lives,
that when people ask about the Kingdom of God
we can point to the quality of our life together.

Love

There is nothing love cannot face; there is no limit to its faith, its hope, its endurance.

~ 1 Corinthians 13:7 ~

Prayer for Reflection

What is it that drives human behaviour?
Greed certainly, ambition too, not to mention fear.
Yet for many it is love that is in the driving seat:
    health professionals;
    mothers, marriage partners, politicians even;
    people who go into the firing line for aid agencies;
    rescue workers, reformers.
Truly, love does make the world go round.

Behind it, Lord, is your love
which embraces the whole world,
and all its awkward people.
Help me today to reflect that love.

Prayer on Today's Theme

Give hope, O Lord,
to those whose endurance is stretched to its limit,

the parent with the fractious child,
the child with the difficult parent,
the employee who is exploited but fears losing her job,
the volunteer whose willingness is taken for granted.
Challenge those who never see things through,
who give in when things don't go their way.

Help us all to fix our eyes on Jesus,
who lived beyond love's limits,
who knew faith from both sides,
who endured to the end
to become our living hope.

River Crossing

As soon as the priests stepped into the river, the water stopped flowing.

~ Joshua 3:15–16 ~

Living God,
if we never go down into the valley
and get our feet wet as we step into the river,
then we will never know what it is to risk everything,
and trust everything to your promises.

If we never go down into the valley
and face the Jordan getting our feet wet,
then we will never know what it is to imperil our faith,
and discover, deeper still, the certainty of love.

If we never stand by the water and get our feet wet,
then we will never know what it is to place all things in
    your hands,
and be held completely by you.

May we step into the water and reach the other side:
into all conflict and cross towards peace;
into all hunger and cross towards the table;
into all injustice and cross towards full living.

Readings

Exodus 14:22–9	*The parting of the Red Sea*
Joshua 3:1–17	*Crossing the Jordan*
Psalm 22:1–11	*Trusting God*
Mark 6:45–52	*Calming of the storm*

Prayer Activity

Today as you journey, to work, to the shops, to visit someone, or even as you go from room to room in your own home, consider the crossing points – doorways, pavement edges, the change from bed to floor, bus to pavement, steps – and pause at each. Feel God's blessing as God crosses with you.

Abundance

He restores my soul.
He leads me in right paths for his name's sake.

~ Psalm 23:3 ~

God,
you make us;
you give to us something new,
something better and stronger and lasting.
And yet we look for you in the old,
speaking of you in words
that our mouths churn out without thinking,
words we expect to have to say,
words we think have to be sung and heard.

But, God, you are alive.
Should we not be amazed that you provide all that we need
    each day?
Should we not find it overwhelming that you offer
    abundance, renewal and constancy in our lives?
Should we not feel your word tingling in our bones,
surging through our veins as you live with us
and in us and remind us of life's essence?

Surely goodness and mercy
will follow us all the days of our lives as we follow you?
Surely you are all we need?   AMEN.

Readings

Psalm 23; John 14:1–8

Silence

Prayer Activity

I shall want nothing. God renews life within me. Read Psalm 23 again, notice which image or picture today renews your life so that you want nothing. Stay with that image for at least five minutes, letting your body, mind and spirit rest, be nurtured, feel, taste, touch and smell.

Jesus Heals Peter's Mother-in-Law

'So he took her by the hand; the fever left her ...'

~ Matthew 8:15 ~

Lord, it seems so simple, so natural,
a wee touch from you and all is well.
There are friends whom I would love to see restored,
up and about again — a wee touch from you?

Minor ailments, recurring problems, terminal illness, a wee
    touch from you?

Your touch demonstrated the power of a life lived in God.
Transforming.

My touch can be less dynamic,
hesitant, with small faith;
embarrassed,
but
with potential.

Free me to be willing to pray
and identify with others by touch,

knowing that I may be a channel of divine grace
and human care appropriately expressed.

We pray for those whose experience of touch is painful and
    unloving
and whose lives are blighted because of this.   AMEN.

Readings

Matthew 8:14–17; Mark 9:38–41; Philippians 2:25–30

Silence

Prayer Activity

Place a hand or hands on yourself wherever you have pain,
tension or stress. (If you cannot reach, use your imagination!)
Or recall any situation or thought which pains you. Relax,
let your breath flow in and out; breathe in the Holy Spirit,
breathe out your pain. Pray.

Lord's Prayer

Cana

On the third day, there was a wedding in Cana of Galilee.

~ John 2:1 ~

Lord, I picture you dancing at the wedding:
no dour onlooker,
frowning in self-righteous judgement, no hide-bound kill-
    joy,
disapproving of such frivolity.

Rather, you were in your element, revelling in the
    celebration.

But then,
joy is your natural element.
This is who you are:
the wellspring and source of all joy,
bringing the swirling colours
of your Kingdom dance
into the grey funereal shabbiness of our respectable
    religion.

You come to change, to transform and to transfigure,
that what we are might give way to what you would have
    us become.

Today I think of all for whom the life of faith
is grey and shabby, bland, watery and joyless.

May they know you present
as the One who dances at weddings.

Prayer Activity

What do you want to ask Jesus to transform? What in your
life is bland, watery or joyless? Jesus came to bring abundant
life. Ask for what you want with passion and clarity. Then,
like Mary, leave it with him. Ask that you may recognise his
answer to you.

Rising

In his great mercy by the resurrection of Jesus Christ from the dead, he gave us new birth into a living hope.

~ 1 Peter 1:3 ~

Prayer for Reflection

It is hard to rise from bed, Lord,
when rudely awakened by the shrill call of the alarm.
It is hard to rise from tradition, Lord,
when challenged to rise to new opportunities to serve you.
It is hard to rise from selfishness, Lord,
when commanded to love my neighbour as myself.

Prayer on Today's Theme

We remember those who cannot rise today:
bedridden at home or in hospital,
sitting in chairs in homes for the elderly
or in hospital wards;
those who cannot get beyond their front door,
    because they are too infirm,
    or afraid of going outside,
    scared about what others might say if they saw them.

God, we thank you for the rising of Jesus from the tomb,
that we may rise with him to newness of life.
We give thanks that with him
each new day is a small resurrection,
with its opportunity to live for you.

Rock Solid

*Whoever hears these words of mine and acts on them is like a man
who had the sense to build his house on rock.*

~ Matthew 7:24 ~

Prayer for Reflection

Let me reflect with you, Lord,
on what I have learned ...
and how I have grown ...;
on what I have discovered about myself ...
and what I now realise about you ...

Breathe on me, breath of God.
Let me know how much I am rooted on the rock,
    whose name is Jesus,
and how much more of me
    has still to be embedded in him.

Prayer on Today's Theme

For the good government
of this land I pray,
that through the Queen or President,
through parliament,

through local councils, justice and decency in public life
may be preserved, and the earthly preconditions be laid
for that quality of life
embodied in Christ's kingdom.

Advise us when we deliberate on politics
and vote for candidates,
that we may act
not according to our latest whim,
but with your will for the world in our minds
and the needs of the world before our eyes.

Inform our judgements,
redeem our passions,
dispel our apathy;
for you made and love this land
and want it to be ruled wisely and well.

Bartimaeus

Then Jesus said to him, 'What do you want me to do for you?' The
blind man said to him, 'My teacher, let me see again'.

~ Mark 10:51 ~

Before I knew you
there was darkness everywhere
and life was meaningless.
Months and years passed in a blur –
the drudge of daily life seemed pointless.

The day we met for the first time
it felt like the scales had fallen from my eyes
and I could really see for the first time.

Colour filled my sight
and life took on a whole new meaning.
Suddenly, every day became precious;
I looked at the world with new eyes,
your eyes, Lord.

Thank you for making a beautiful world,
thank you for letting me share in it.
Use my eyes, ears, mouth and hands

to make this world a better place –
where we can all enjoy your creation.

Prayer Activity

Close your eyes, and as you sit quietly for a few minutes imagine how you would cope if you were blind. Think about how you would go about your daily life: washing, dressing, cooking, working, etc. Give thanks for people learning to live with a disability.

The Value of Wisdom

The wise get all the knowledge they can, but when fools speak,
trouble is not far off.

~ Proverbs 10:14 ~

Prayer for Reflection

Lord of the ages,
when I delude myself into thinking
that I am growing wiser with the passing years,
help me to question my assumption.

Help me to listen to younger people, and their ideas,
and not to be wearied by their enthusiasm or their endless
   talking
... and this, just in case they may be nearer
   your will for the world
   than I am.

Give me, Lord,
the humility to be reticent where that is needed,
and the sensitivity to speak the truth in kindness.

Prayer on Today's Theme

Loving God,

confront today those who never question

that they might be wrong;

surprise those who stumble through life in slavery to rules
  you never intended;

befriend those who believe you have the truth and are keen
  to find it.

Laughing

... a time to weep, and a time to laugh.

~ Ecclesiastes 3:4 ~

Prayer for Reflection

There are times when I feel happy:
just being with friends can make me laugh in pure joy;
thank you, God, for the blessing of shared laughter.
It is your gift too that I can laugh at myself,
at my quaint and quirky ways,
at the daft things I say and do.

Prayer for Today

Thank you, God,
for those who are the life and soul of the party,
for those whose sense of humour is infectious,
for those who are just a good laugh,
for laughter's cleansing power.

Thank you, God,
for laughing at us,
for poking fun at our pomposity,
for bursting the balloon of the unco guid.

Lord,
you give us the gift of laughter;
help us to share our laughter with others,
to lighten their lives as well as our own.

Joy

Let hope keep you joyful; in trouble stand firm; persist in prayer.

~ Romans 12:12 ~

Prayer for Reflection

Why is it so disconcerting
    to find joy in a list of Christian duties?
Am I so convinced that being a Christian consists
    in a number of unwelcome responsibilities?
Surely joy is for off-duty moments
    when we lay aside our hair shirts
    and let our hair down!

Yet, Lord, perhaps the quality of my joy
is the real test of Christian seriousness.
Is not joy the emotion which comes
    when body, mind and spirit
    all fall into place,
    each nourishing the other?

Help me, Lord, to tell the difference
between the superficial joyousness
that fades when trouble comes

and true Christian joy
which bubbles up through suffering
and relives the triumph of Easter.

Prayer on Today's Theme

Risen Christ,
visit those whose eyes are haunted with suffering
and help them laugh again;
challenge those who laugh at others' expense,
and help them face their own pain;

stir those who cannot let themselves go
and release in them the joy that lies confined;

give to your Church new songs and fresh voices
that its joy in you may sound throughout the earth.

Joy and Laughter

Then our mouth was filled with laughter, and our tongue with shouts of joy; then it was said among the nations, 'The Lord has done great things for them'.

~ Psalm 126:2 ~

What kind of laughter have you made, God?
People laugh in disgust, to scoff,
we laugh when the tension is just too much.
Some laugh at their schemes and plans, excited by their
    cunning.
And we laugh in the face of criticism to show we don't take
    it seriously.
But it is the best medicine.
We enjoy a good laugh with family and friends.
Some things are so funny, we are amused, we can't help it.
We love to laugh after feeling low –
it lifts us up, we feel better.
Surely God, this is what you made laughter for
– excitement at good news,
– delight in company and shared experience,
– joy at the unexpected; the kind of joy that Mary felt as
    her world turned upside down that first Easter morning,
        the kind of joy a baby can bring,
the kind of joy that love brings beyond pain:

– joy that can't be contained, that just bursts out
like laughter.

So today God,
may I not take myself too seriously,
may I see the funny side,
and may I make someone smile, even laugh, for your
    sake.   AMEN.

Prayer Activity

Think about someone or something that makes you laugh or
think of some good news you have recently heard. Smile to
God as a prayer and give thanks for God's uplifting spirit.

The Happy Life

Happy are those …

~ Psalm 1:1 ~

Lord! What a beautiful way to start
a book of songs: 'Happy is the one.'
We often start with negative-sounding words: sinner, duty,
   effort, rules,
so we struggle long for a happy ending.

God! What an exuberant image of life:
'A tree planted by water channels;
It yields its fruit in season
And its foliage never fails.'
I can picture it: leafy, fruit-bearing, a seasonal life.

Lord, who are the wicked you have in mind?
Foes who endanger life? Enemies within? Pride, greed, lust,
   fear?
When these threaten life, help me to see them in *your*
   perspective –
'like chaff driven by the wind'.

Lord, let my life have the powerful focus of delight in all
    that is good,
your 'Law' no duty imposed but a happiness
    within.   AMEN.

Readings

Psalm 1; Psalm 19; John 15:1–17; Romans 13:10; Galatians
5:14

Prayer Activity

Think of your life as a tree and draw a picture of it. Place
around its roots the things that promote life and happiness,
e.g. faith, friends, a book, a musical instrument, whatever
is life enhancing to you. Explore the significance for you,
today, of this image.

Blessing

    Turn the wandering desires of your heart to God,
    feed the roots of your life with love,
    fill your soul with happiness.
    And so, let your tree of life bear much fruit,
    in God, in Christ, in Spirit.   AMEN.

A Calm Mind

Peace of mind makes the body healthy, but jealousy is like a cancer.

~ Proverbs 14:30 ~

Prayer for Reflection

A prayer for a calm sough
for me, please, Lord;

for me when I fret, and worry, and imagine the worst;
for me when I think the birds have it easy
and forget that He who sees the sparrows is also watching
   me.

My care at your feet,
my stress on your yoke,
my mind stayed on Jesus.

Prayer on Today's Theme

In a society
where we envy what we don't have,
and encourage each other's jealousy
until, in body or mind,

we drop like flies;
in such a society,
we need your maladjustment, Jesus.

Tread the path of simplicity
through our complicated lives,
until we see and cherish
the peace
at the centre of the storm.

Beach – Dawning

Jesus said to them, 'Come and eat.'
~ John 21:12 ~

The new dawn shakes itself awake,
pulling apart the night with yellows and golds;
and in the freshness of this thin light,
the beach seems crowded with resurrection.

Hereon the edge of things:
between shore and land;
between dark and light;
between home and adventure;
I meet you face to face,
and staring into eyes
that confront me with images of crucifixion and death,
of darkness and things unimaginable,

I can see beyond,
as you have done,
into a reflection clear with the new promise of eternity,
and with sand between my toes,
the smell of fish on my fingers,

spray on my face,
and salt in my mouth,
we share a makeshift breakfast –
a sacramental moment,
that builds with light, and truth,
and love,
for in my heart I know you are alive!

May every morsel I share with the world this day,
contain as much Good News as this.

Prayer Activity

Be there on that beach. Feel the smells and the sounds, the sun
or wind on your face. Take yourself towards a small beach-fire
and there is Jesus preparing breakfast. Eat with him. What
would you say to him? What does he say to you?

Acceptance

Here I am! Send me.

~ Isaiah 6:8 ~

Prayer for Reflection

I'm not much to look at, Lord.
I don't always get things right, either.
What on earth do you see in me?

And yet you call me by name and lead me out!
Wonderfully, miraculously, I am made in your image!
Praise be!
Let me remember with joy and humility
    that you love me just as I am.

Prayer on Today's Theme

O God,
be with all whose spirit is always striving
    for the unreachable and unattainable,
who are always crying for the moon
    or grieving over spilt milk.

Be with those who refuse
to accept the constraints of their circumstances –
    the prisoner in the cell,
    the patient in the ward,
    the paraplegic in the wheelchair –
    that they may press on to achieve what seems
    impossible.